THE
INTUITION
PACK

THE
INTUITION
PACK

CRAIG
HAMILTON-PARKER

A GODSFIELD BOOK

First published in Great Britain in 2000
by Godsfield Press Ltd.
A division of David and Charles Ltd.
Laurel House, Station Approach,
New Alresford, Hants SO24 9JH, UK

10 9 8 7 6 5 4 3 2 1

© Godsfield Press 2000
Text © Craig Hamilton-Parker 2000

Designed for Godsfield Press by
The Bridgewater Book Company

ILLUSTRATOR *Kim Glass*
PHOTOGRAPHER *Ian Parsons*
except as listed below

The publishers are grateful to the following
for permission to reproduce copyright material:
Ian Bellamy: page 10
Tony Stone Images: pages 14, 32, 33, 37, 65
The Image Bank: page 21
Telegraph Colour Library: page 39

ISBN 1–84181–007–X

Manufactured in China

Craig Hamilton-Parker's website is at http://www.psychics.co.uk

Contents

Part 1: **What is the Intuition?** 6

The hidden powers of the intuition 8

Intuitive discoveries 10

Extrasensory perception 12

Unlocking the unconscious 14

Philosophy and the intuition 16

Are you intuitive? 18

The inkblot test 20

Understanding the unconscious 22

Projecting the unconscious mind 24

Seers and scrying 26

A child's eye 28

Oracles 30

Part 2: **Working with the Cards** 34

Improving your ability to "see" 36

Preparing to use the cards 38

Experiment 1: Tuning in to your intuition 40

The meaning of symbols 42

Symbols and the mind 44

Symbols and your experience 46

Experiment 2: Programming your intuition 48

Experiment 3: Recalling and interpreting
dreams 52

Experiment 4: Overcoming creative blocks 56

Using the cards in everyday life 60

Accessing your extrasensory perception 62

Experiment 5: Predicting the future 64

Reading the cards for others 68

Receiving thoughts 70

Past, present, and future reading 72

Designing your own spreads 74

Developing the inner voice 76

Part 3: **Dictionary of Symbols** 78

People, faces, and parts of the body 80

Creatures 84

Places and objects 88

Myths and magic 92

Suggested reading 94

Index 95

Part 1

....

WHAT IS THE INTUITION?

According to a dictionary, intuition is "immediate mental apprehension without reasoning; immediate insight" (Collins, 10th edition, London, 1990). It's something that we all take for granted, yet isn't it remarkable how often we can come to correct conclusions without having all the facts at hand or using reason? How is it that we can immediately assess some people the first time we meet them, and find that our initial insight is correct? And why can we sometimes guess which direction to travel in, or the correct answer to a question? What gives us these immediate insights?

Behind our normal consciousness lies the vast, untapped world of the unconscious, where billions of memories and incredible, unused skills are locked away. Every one of us is

6

a secret genius. The unconscious is capable of amazing creativity, inventiveness, and mental agility. For example, experiments with hypnosis have shown that it is possible to remember just about anything. Things that are "impossible" to remember in normal circumstances – such as what you had for lunch on May 14th, 1984 – can be recalled with perfect clarity during a hypnotic trance. All of this knowledge is hidden in the unconscious and can be utilized if we allow our intuition to do its job. We all possess intuition, but for most people it remains a mysterious force, working just when they least expect it to.

The Intuition Pack will enable you to make the best of your creative faculties. It will train your intuition for use in everyday situations, and help you to come to terms with your emotional side. You will find out how to use the cards to uncover creative solutions to problems, to stimulate ideas, and to give you insight into your dreams and the unconscious processes of the psyche. You will even discover how to get in touch with the psychic side of yourself and your higher spiritual self through your intuition.

> All our interior world is reality – and that perhaps more so than our apparent world
>
> MARC CHAGALL

The Hidden Powers of the Intuition

....

TO ATTUNE to your intuition, you will need to become more aware of the psychological forces that lie below the surface of the conscious mind. You must listen to your inner voice, trust your hunches, and pay careful attention to the content of your dreams. If you do this, you will achieve harmony within yourself and unlock creative powers that you've never realized you possess.

DREAM POWER

The hidden power of the intuition often reveals itself in dreams. The intuition is at work while we sleep and can sometimes offer solutions to problems through the imagery of dreams. During the day, your unconscious mind notices things about people and situations, and will bring this to your attention in a dream. For example, you might meet a friend, then later that evening dream about the friend being ill. Though you noticed nothing wrong

8

with your friend at the meeting, your unconscious may have observed telltale signs of illness – the tone of the complexion, an imperceptible odor, or a slight quiver in the voice. These subtle signals may be brought to your attention during sleep, when the intuition is allowed to function.

SPONTANEOUS GUIDANCE

In many cases the intuition provides us with information that we cannot possibly have known otherwise. The most obvious example is an intuitive glimpse of the future. Thousands of examples of precognition and clairvoyance have been documented – cases on record include people who dreamed of disasters such as the Chernobyl nuclear accident, or that Princess Diana would die. Others claim to have chosen a winning horse, or found the location of a lost object through a dream.

When we are awake, the unconscious mind can interrupt our conscious thinking. It may note something about someone's tone of voice or body language, warning us that the person is not quite what he or she seems. This is why our gut feelings about people so often prove to be correct. As you work with *The Intuition Pack*, pay attention to the way your intuition functions in everyday life. Do you listen to your hunches and trust your gut feelings? Intuitive people are always open to the prompting of the unconscious. You too can make using your intuition part of your daily life.

Imagination is the eye of the soul

JOSEPH JOUBERT

Intuitive Discoveries

....

SOME OF the greatest minds have trusted their intuition to help them solve difficult intellectual problems. During the day the conscious, rational mind is in complete control of our life, and we do things for logical reasons. At night the intuition breaks through the stranglehold of reason and forces ideas upon us that we could never arrive at by logical thought alone.

THE SEWING MACHINE

Many great inventions are the result of intuition, of "sleeping on" a problem. For example, the sewing machine

owes its existence to a dream. Its inventor, Elias Howe, was stuck for a solution for a working model. One night he dreamed that a savage king ordered him to invent a sewing machine. When Howe said that he'd tried but couldn't, the king's tribe raised their spears to kill him. Just before the

fateful moment, Howe noticed that each spear had a hole in it just above the point. This provided the vital clue that led to the commercial perfection of his sewing-machine model.

ATOMIC PHYSICS

Atomic physics owes one of its fundamental discoveries to the intuitive insight of a dream. The Danish physicist Niels Bohr, while trying to understand the nature of the atom, dreamed of a sun composed of burning gases with planets orbiting it, attached to fine threads. When he woke, he realized that this solved his puzzle – it explained the structure of the atom, heralding the birth of atomic physics.

The unconscious is like an incredible inner computer that continually solves problems for us in the background of our normal awareness. When it has done its work, the answers appear in our head as if from nowhere. This "eureka" effect has influenced people from just about every profession, including artists and military generals as well as inventors and scientists.

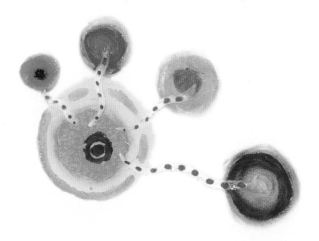

Genius, in truth, means little more than the faculty of perceiving in an unhabitual way

WILLIAM JAMES

Extrasensory Perception

···

THROUGH THE intuition we can access the powers of extra-sensory perception (ESP) – a term coined by the American scientist Joseph Banks Rhine, and a subject that we will study in more detail later in this book. ESP refers to any mental faculty that allows a person to acquire information about the world without the use of the known senses. It is broken down into the categories listed below.

TELEPATHY

The ability to "tune in" to the thoughts of others or to inject your own thoughts into another's mind.

If you know who's calling before you answer the phone, you may have picked up someone else's thoughts. Telepathy takes no notice of distance. Your friend could be calling from Australia and you'll still pick up the mental signals. Edgar D. Mitchell, an astronaut on board Apollo 14, even conducted a telepathy experiment with a "sender" on earth as he winged his way to the moon!

CLAIRVOYANCE

The power to see things that are not available to you through the known senses and are not known to anyone else.

Some people have an amazing sense of direction and can find their way around without maps or signs. They just "know" which way to go. Other people can sense water, either by dowsing with rods or by holding their hands over maps. Perhaps you've helped someone find a missing object. You suddenly had a hunch about its location and were proved right. If this has happened to you, you may

have used clairvoyance to find this information, even if you didn't know you were doing it.

PRECOGNITION

The skill of looking into the future and seeing events before they take place.

Your intuitive gifts may have given you a hunch about a winning horse, or even the winning numbers of a lottery. For example, a man from Portsmouth, UK, knew he was going to win a prize the day before he bought a lottery ticket. He even announced it to his friends. The next day he won £50,000 (about $80,000)!

PSYCHOKINESIS

The use of the power of the mind to influence matter (to move objects by thought, for example).

You may think that you cannot possibly have this power, but have you noticed how machinery breaks down when you're angry or upset? How the telephone goes on the blink during an argument, or the fax machine jams as soon as there's a deadline? You may be having an effect on your environment through your psychic energy.

> If you can look into the seeds of time and say, which grain will grow, and which will not, speak then to me

WILLIAM SHAKESPEARE (MACBETH)

Unlocking the Unconscious

IF YOU GAZE at any random pattern, you are soon likely to start seeing faces and other pictures within its haphazard forms. Many people claim that they can see a face in the shadows of Mars, or in the patterns on the moon's surface. Similarly, you may notice that when you look at the coals of a fire, the patterns in sand, a rock formation, or the gnarled bark of a tree, pictures are revealed in their shapes.

ACCESS THE INTUITION

There are many ways to access the intuition. In particular, play and imagination bring us close to this creative source. Pursuits such as music and painting put us in touch with our intuitive powers. When you deal with other people, your intuitive self forms unconscious judgments based on your subliminal perception of their facial expressions or voice tones. This is obvious between mother and child. How do you know that your baby is about to wake, or that he is disturbed when left with a babysitter? It is because of the supersensitive perception – or the paranormal insight – of the intuition.

CHILD'S EYE

As a child you probably gazed at white cumulus clouds drifting in the blue sky and noticed how they formed into the fantastic shapes of faces, animals, and spectacular landscapes. These changing images come from the unconscious and are

14

projected onto the random cloud shapes by the mind. The pictures that you see reveal hidden processes deep within you – the thoughts generated by your innermost self. It's a form of daydreaming, and just like the symbols in a dream, the pictures are keys to the secrets of the mind.

SEEING SHAPES

The images reflect the processes of your unconscious and reveal a great deal about your hopes, fears, and emotions. In addition, psychic people claim that, just like dreams, these symbolic images can occasionally contain messages about the future.

Shortly before his death in 1977, Elvis Presley stood gazing into the sky above Graceland. He looked sullen and worried, and is said to have confided in his friends that he could see his own death forecast in the clouds passing by.

Psychics use random shapes formed by tea leaves, hot coals, smoke, or the flaws in a crystal ball to project images from their intuition (*see pages 30 to 33*). You too can get into the habit of seeing pictures in random shapes. You could even make up a game with a friend to find out who can see the most pictures in the clouds, a coal fire, or even the trees when out walking in the woods.

The sky is the daily bread of the eyes

RALPH WALDO EMERSON

Philosophy and the Intuition

·······································

MYSTICS AND scientists have different views about what the intuition is and how it works. Biologists, psychologists, and philosophers have all attempted to understand and explain the intuitive process. The subject is inevitably controversial, because most intuitive experiences are subjective and not repeatable in the laboratory. It is perhaps the philosophers who come closest to understanding intuition.

REASON AND INTUITION

Some theories about ancient times have claimed that successful societies used intuition in favor of reason.

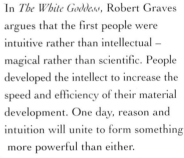

In *The White Goddess*, Robert Graves argues that the first people were intuitive rather than intellectual – magical rather than scientific. People developed the intellect to increase the speed and efficiency of their material development. One day, reason and intuition will unite to form something more powerful than either.

Scientists, psychologists, and philosophers have attempted to reduce the intuitive process to something empirical. Scientists have proposed that intuition is the brain's capacity for subconscious computation.

Others consider it to be the result of collective habits and social conditioning. Some biologists propose that intuition is part of a biological instinct – for example, the salmon uses intuition to locate its spawning ground.

Philosophers have also attempted to explain the intuition. Immanuel Kant maintained that it is through intuition that we construct and maintain the basic elements of our world. He claimed that our sense of space and time, our sense of identity, our sense of beauty and goodness, and our sense of the truth of things are all founded on our intuitive understanding rather than our reason.

INTUITION OVER REASON

Philosophers state that intuition is superior to perception and reasoning. It is the function that enables us to understand the world. Similarly, in linguistics, listeners are thought to recognize the meaning of words and sentences through the intuition. Intuition is the quality that brings everything together. We may be born with a certain amount of intuitive knowledge; for example, developmental psychologists have documented the existence of both spatial awareness and "innate grammar" in infants before they could have learned these skills through social conditioning.

All of these ideas are valuable, but they do not acknowledge the mysterious nature of the intuition and its apparent paranormal qualities. Clearly, the word "intuition" means different things to different people.

> There are no facts, only interpretations
>
> FRIEDRICH NIETZSCHE

Are You Intuitive?

....

YOU ALREADY use your powers of intuition in everyday life. Contemplating *how* you use them will identify the nature of your powers and provide a solid basis for developing them further. The more you think about the intuitive side of yourself, the more these psychological powers will emerge within you, so take some time to consider the questions below.

HOW WOULD YOU DEFINE INTUITION?

Perhaps you would describe it as "knowing" without being able to explain how you know. You may choose words such as "gut feeling," "insight," or "hunch." Perhaps you heard or saw something "leap out" or "come out of the blue," or perhaps you had a "flash" of inspiration. Think of the specific occasions on which you have used these terms.

CAN YOU REMEMBER AN INTUITIVE EXPERIENCE?

You may be able to recall an insight that "came out of nowhere." Think about what your first impressions were when you first met people you know now. Did your "gut feelings" later prove to be correct or did you misjudge people? Ask yourself whether you truly experienced an intuitive insight, or whether you were reacting out of prejudice or preconceived opinions about the person.

WHEN DOES YOUR INTUITION WORK BEST?

It is possible that you are a good judge of character and quickly experience intuitive insights about the people you meet. Maybe you get hunches at work. Do you feel at your most intuitive when working on creative projects? Maybe you are good at preempting children's needs.

DO YOU TRUST YOUR INTUITION?

How do you feel when you make a decision based upon your intuition? Perhaps you think it's foolish to be so rash. Many people feel confident when they obey the prompting of an "inner voice" or follow what the heart tells them. Are there any occasions when you should have trusted your intuition? Perhaps you can think of times when your intuition was completely wrong.

WHICH SENSES DO YOU USE WITH YOUR INTUITION?

Do you see a picture in your mind's eye? Perhaps you hear an inner voice. Some people get a nasty metallic taste in the mouth when they are warned by their intuition. Does your intuition work through your emotions? Perhaps you notice some changes in your bodily functions when your intuition is at work, such as a rise in temperature or shakiness in the limbs.

WHAT MOTIVATES YOUR INTUITION?

For some people the intuition is a protective force that warns them when a situation is dangerous, or when they are likely to be tricked by someone. Has your intuition seen through a lie? Is your intuition a conscience that guides you, or is it influenced by guilt?

HAVE YOU EXPERIENCED PSYCHIC INTUITION?

Perhaps you dreamed of the future, or knew who was calling as soon as the telephone rang. Have your hunches about how schoolmates would do in life proved to be correct? Perhaps you have felt that a tragedy would befall someone, and it did. Perhaps you had a feeling about a good thing, and that happened too!

The Inkblot Test

I N T H E E A R L Y P A R T of the 20th century, in Switzerland, Hermann Rorschach developed a psychological test by experimenting with a set of cards showing symmetrical inkblots. He asked psychiatric patients to interpret the shapes and used the results to identify personality traits and disorders. Today, the Rorschach test is considered to be one of the world's best psychodiagnostic procedures.

THE INKBLOT IDEA

Rorschach was born on November 8th, 1884, in Zurich, Switzerland. His father was a painter and he considered the same career before opting to study psychiatry at Eugen Bleuler's clinic in Zurich. Rorschach's idea came while he was working in a Swiss psychiatric hospital with adolescents. He noticed that certain children gave characteristically different answers to a popular game known as Blotto (*Klecksographie*), which involved looking at inkblots to find out who could see the most interesting pictures in the random shapes. It struck Rorschach that what the children were seeing revealed a great deal about their psychological condition. From this simple game he devised the Rorschach test, now an indispensable tool of psychiatry.

Rorschach himself had little success with his theories. He had difficulties finding a publisher for his book, *Psychodiagnostik*, which outlined his ideas, and when it did come out in 1921 it was not well received. He died of appendicitis in 1922 at the age of 37, having invested just under four years of work in his inkblot test, but it was to become perhaps the single most powerful psychometric instrument ever envisioned.

DEVELOPING
THE TECHNIQUES

By the 1930s, interest in the Rorschach techniques had spread across Europe and the United States. A great deal of controversy arose about how best to use the cards, and different schools evolved with sometimes diametrically opposed ideas. The European schools, guided by the Danish-Swiss psychologist Ewald Bohm, tried to keep as close as possible to Rorschach's original concept. In America, the cards were being used in a number of ways, until eventually, in 1960, John E. Exner pioneered an alternative system – a synthesis of all the different systems. The Exner school is now the dominant methodology.

In spirit, the Bohm and Exner systems are very similar. Both use complicated scoring and specific interpretations for each shape and area of the inkblots. To understand and apply the Rorschach systems takes considerable training and expertise. In addition, the cards used by psychiatrists are printed from the original plates, which are now 75 years old. Each reprinting requires great attention and is made on what can now only be regarded as ancient equipment. Even the weather is taken into account: if it is too humid, or too dry, the printing process is rescheduled. However, these processes ensure that the prints are virtually identical reproductions of the originals.

Though the idea is similar, the methods taught in *The Intuition Pack*, the cards used, and the objectives of its techniques are completely different from those used by Rorschach and his successors.

21

Understanding the Unconscious

....

HERMANN RORSCHACH wasn't the first to look for and interpret shapes in inkblots. Leonardo da Vinci in the 15th century and German poet Justinus Kerner in the 19th both used inkblots to inspire creativity and stimulate ideas. Their more recent use as a psychological tool has been based on the belief that they draw out the unconscious mind, which psychologists believe holds the key to problems.

FREUD'S "LEVELS OF THE MIND"

Sigmund Freud (1856–1939) coined the term "psychoanalysis" to describe his methods for curing the mental problems of his patients. He believed that most of these were caused by sexual difficulties that were repressed into areas of the mind that we are unaware of. Freud used the analogy of an iceberg floating in water to describe this hidden part of us. The top seventh poking above the surface of the water represents our conscious mind – our conscious awareness when we are awake. The surface of the water is the boundary between the conscious mind and the unconscious mind. Freud called this the "preconscious." This boundary contains material accessible to the conscious mind, such as facts, memories, ideas, and motives. It disguises the information coming from the unconscious by changing it into symbolism, so that we will not be disturbed by what our unconscious is really thinking.

Below the preconscious lies the largest part of the mind, which Freud called the "personal unconscious." This six-sevenths contains our secret wishes and fears as well as the traumatic memories of the past. It stores repressed emotions and unacknowledged urges. It is the uncontrolled, instinctive side of us. Freud believed that these thoughts were hidden and unavailable to us.

COLLECTIVE UNCONSCIOUS

Between 1907 and 1913, Carl Gustav Jung (1875–1961), Freud's star pupil, fell out with his tutor and proposed a new theory of the unconscious. Freud had recognized that the unconscious could retain "daily residues" – images of our daily life that had been forgotten. But Jung noticed that some of his patients expressed themselves with imagery from ancient traditions. He wondered if the unconscious could hold "archaic residues." His patients were using inherited imagery, buried in the unconscious mind.

In 1919 Jung called these images "archetypes." He also proposed that we have a "collective unconscious"

formed of instincts and archetypes. The archetypes, inborn forms of intuition that are the necessary determinants of all psychic processes, manifest as images. They are primordial ideas and are numinous – charged with a sense of the sacred. Many of the images you will see in the Intuition Cards are archetypal symbols originating from the collective unconscious. They are powerful images, representing the innermost processes of your psyche.

Projecting the Unconscious Mind

....

THE POWER of intuition is so strong in some people that it causes hallucinations as images from their unconscious are projected into the world around them. It is very common for these visions to occur on waking from a dream. For thousands of years, clairvoyants and psychics have used these visual projection techniques as a method for accessing their psychic powers.

CRYSTAL GAZING

The best-known projection technique is crystallomancy – crystal gazing. The Mayans, Incas, Native North Americans, Australian aborigines, and many tribal societies throughout the world have used crystal gazing. It came to Europe in about the 5th century and was a very popular pursuit during the Victorian era. Today, there is a massive resurgence of interest in crystals, crystal healing, and crystal gazing.

THE CRYSTAL BALL

The crystal ball is the classic tool of the clairvoyant. Many occultists believe that it is the oldest method of precognition, which existed even before the invention of writing. Today, people use the same techniques to induce visions as they did centuries ago. The practitioner makes his or her mind as blank as

24

possible and gazes into the center of the crystal. The crystal may appear to turn cloudy, and out of this white blur, scenes, images, and faces emerge. Sometimes these pictures are static, like a photograph, and sometimes they are dynamic, like images on a miniature television.

In the same way that you saw pictures in the clouds when you were a child, when crystal gazing you access the unconscious mind by projecting imagery onto white shapes. By carefully noting what he or she sees, the clairvoyant will interpret the images as glimpses of the future, or as a way of getting to know the unconscious mind better. Sometimes these techniques can reveal startling predictions.

SCRYING

Divination by gazing into a reflective surface – scrying – is perhaps the most accurate form of prediction that there is. Crystal gazing is a form of scrying. It has links with

hydromancy – divination by water – because water and other liquids were once the only reflective materials available to most people.

These methods took advantage of the mind's ability to project images from the unconscious onto a surface or into reflective material. Often sacred pools or springs were used as well as fonts or bowls of "holy" water. The Babylonians are known to have gazed into bowls of water to divine the future. The Egyptians used a pool of ink held in the hand, and the Hindus gazed at bowls of molasses. The widespread practice of scrying brought fame to the greatest seers.

Seers and Scrying

GAZING INTO A REFLECTIVE surface in order to divine the future was used by most of the great seers whose predictions have stood the test of time. This technique – scrying – was often used in conjunction with astrology. Nostradamus and John Dee are two famous seers from history, both of whom used scrying to look into the future. The prophecies of Nostradamus are still with us today.

NOSTRADAMUS

Perhaps the most famous seer to use scrying to prophesy was the French physician and astrologer Michel de Notredame (1503–66), better known as Nostradamus. Although Nostradamus explained his predictions in astrological terms, most of his prophecies were obtained by scrying and dated afterward using astrology. He prophesied the Great Fire of London in 1666, the French Revolution, Napoleon's defeat at Waterloo, the nuclear bombs at Hiroshima and Nagasaki, and many more harrowing events yet to come.

Nostradamus's technique involved gazing into a bowl of water resting on a brass tripod. Here, in the candlelit waters, he would see visions of the future, which he noted down in quatrains (four-line verses) in a mixture of Old French and Latin. To add to the mystery, perhaps, and to protect himself from possible persecution by the Church, he then coded his work. He added words of his own invention, replaced names with initials and nicknames, and filled his work with puns and anagrams.

JOHN DEE

One of the strangest scryers, John Dee (1527–1608), was an acclaimed English mathematician, and astrologer to Mary Tudor. With the help of his assistant, Edward Kelly, he used scrying in combination with a complicated system of numbers to communicate with the angels. According to Dee, an angel would appear in the center of the crystal ball. She would then point in sequence to numbers and letters on a chart. Dee called the language of these communications "Enochian" and described it in his diaries, *Quinti Libri Mysteriorum* (Sloane manuscript 3188, British Library). Of course, many skeptics have said that his work is all nonsense and fantasy, but find it difficult to explain the strange fact that the "Enochian" language has a consistent grammar and syntax.

The Intuition Cards in this pack can be used in a similar way to the methods of Nostradamus and Dee. The techniques you will learn with the cards are a form of scrying, but they are much easier to master than the crystal ball. Instead of projecting the imagery from the unconscious onto the formless glass of the crystal, the inkblots easily take on the shapes and pictures that the psychic intuition is trying to reveal. They are a means of accessing the supernormal powers of the unconscious, and in the right hands, they may reveal the secrets of destiny.

A Child's Eye

··

NOT EVERYBODY can tap the unconscious or clairvoyant powers by scrying with water, crystal, glass, or mirrors. However, most people can see a face or pictures in crumpled clothes, clouds, or a blot of ink. As a child you may have found it easy to see pictures and shapes in the things around you. As you became an adult this ability may have been lost. Learning to see the world again through a child's eyes is key.

VISUAL PROJECTION

For many people, scrying and crystal gazing are very difficult methods to master. It is uncomfortable to sit with watering eyes gazing into glass or crystal. For most, there are no results after months of patient sitting. It is not known why some people experience results using scrying and others struggle hopelessly. It is estimated that only about one person in twenty is psychically sensitive enough to get results with this method. Some psychologists believe that this ability has nothing to do with psychic powers at all – that crystal gazing is only a way of inducing visual hallucinations similar to the hypnagogic imagery seen by some people between sleeping and waking. Psychics argue that the imagery is generated by the unconscious, which also contains the clairvoyant faculty of the mind.

Deliberate visual projection in order to access the intuitive powers is very different from the uncontrolled hallucinations of mental illness. In the latter case, patients lose touch with reality. They fail to distinguish between imagery and perception, and suppose that what they imagine is

HOLDING ON TO REALITY

Macbeth had lost touch with reality.
With the Intuition Cards you can use
the power of visions while keeping
your feet firmly on the ground.
For centuries seers and prophets
have safely used these techniques
to project the contents of the
unconscious mind.

You will learn to use the
incredible powers of your
unconscious without being deceived
by hallucination. At the same time,
you can loosen the iron grip that
reason holds on the world and its
interpretation, and allow your
imagination through.

external and can be seen by others.
Children sometimes fail to make the
distinction, as do people who are in
solitary confinement, or those
responding to an intense emotional
need. Hallucinations evaporate when
the person realizes that others do not
see the world as he or she does.

Shakespeare expresses the nature
of a hallucination perfectly in his
play *Macbeth*. While planning to kill
Duncan, Macbeth sees a vision of a
dagger: "Art thou not, fatal vision,
sensible to feeling as to sight? Or art
thou but a dagger of the mind, a false
creation, proceeding from the heat-
oppressed brain?"

Oracles

·······································

M ANY ORACLES have used random patterns to tell the future. Oenomancy interpreted the patterns made by wine poured out as a gift to the gods; scapulomancy read the patterns of fissures on the burned shoulder-blade bone of an animal; and tephromancy analyzed the ashes of burnt offerings. Even the *I Ching*, the famous Chinese oracle, began by exploring the shapes of cracks in heated tortoise shells.

PYROMANCY

One of the first techniques to take advantage of the mind's ability to form pictures from random shapes was pyromancy – the art of divination from fire. It is thought that fire oracles may have originated in ancient times, when burnt offerings were made to the gods. The ancient seers studied the flames as the sacrifices were made and interpreted auguries and omens from them. The way the smoke rose and its smell and thickness were all considered to be messages from the gods. For example, a clear flame burning without smoke or sound was considered a sign of good fortune.

Other methods of divination performed at the sacrificial pyre used burning leaves, objects thrown into the flames, and the sounds made by casting salt or laurel leaves across the fire. All of these were subject to interpretation and analysis.

Visual-projection techniques were used by shamanic seers to stimulate clairvoyance and seek knowledge of the future. Many of these old techniques survive today, and it is still possible to employ a pyromancer to foretell the future. The technique involves sitting quietly in front of a fire that has died down to a bed of glowing coals and entering a state of relaxed meditation. When the pyromancer is ready, ritual dictates that he should then scatter a handful of salt across the glowing coals. Once the flames and crackling have died down, he gazes into the fire and contemplates the pictures he sees in the glowing shapes for between 10 and 15 minutes.

A number of different pictures may appear, but one usually stands out from the rest as particularly significant. If no image is seen, the pyromancy is abandoned and a new fire is lit 24 hours later. However, if one shape stands out clearly, this is considered to be important and is interpreted as the oracle for the future. It is auspicious if the glow of the coals is particularly strong – this brings good fortune.

Once the symbol from the fire has been determined, it is interpreted according to a set of traditional meanings. For example, a windmill represents a change for the better, as does a fountain, but to see flowers in the coals bodes disappointment. However, the true clairvoyant goes beyond these traditional meanings and listens to the voice of his or her intuition to ascertain the omen's true meaning. From this inner prompting he or she gains a truer precognition.

TASSEOGRAPHY

Tea-leaf reading – tasseography – is a popular technique used to access the intuition through random patterns. The pictures created by the shapes of the leaves are interpreted as oracles for the future.

This method of divination is thought to have originated in ancient China, although the Romans used a similar technique to read the lees of their wine. In fact, for thousands of years, the pattern made by the sediment left in the bottom of any drinking cup has been thought to predict the drinker's future. I know a fortuneteller who predicts the future by reading dirty plates! This method is the same as the traditional methods – he looks for pictures and interprets these as symbols for the future.

GEOMANCY

The ancient art of geomancy is also experiencing a revival. This is divination by interpreting the signs and symbols in the landscape. In Tibet, it was customary for the traveling monk to interpret oracles from the shapes and forms he encountered on his way. The pictures seen in the shape of rocks, or in a mountain's melting ice, all augured the future. Sometimes matters of state would be decided according to the omens seen in the simulacra

observed in rocks and trees, or in the stains on temple walls.

Similarly, in Christian countries, much controversy has centered around images of Christ that have appeared in the stains on flagstones or plaster walls. Today, clairvoyants read the pictures and shapes in a tray of sand as a means of focusing their powers. Increasingly popular, sand-reading is also considered to be an accurate way of predicting the future.

Part 2

WORKING WITH THE CARDS

Part 1 *described the theories that lie at the heart of the techniques employed with the Intuition Cards. As you have seen, cumulus clouds, hot coals, tea leaves, and other random shapes can all be used as a mirror for the imagination, the unconscious, and clairvoyance. By interpreting the pictures as symbols, we understand what our intuition is telling us. On each of the Intuition Cards is a symmetrical inkblot. The many pictures that you see in the forms of the inkblots are the keys to unlocking your psychological and psychic powers.*

Take the cards in your hands and examine them. Already you may notice how the shapes of the ink form into pictures. You will probably see faces first, because these are the most common shapes imposed by the mind on the random swirls of ink. Some of the faces may be weird-looking or distorted. They may be frightening, bizarre, or funny. Sometimes the whole inkblot can form a face, but when your attention shifts, you may notice that

34

what you thought was one face is in fact made up of many other faces. Sometimes faces merge together or appear to interact or be part of a theatrical scene or situation. Enjoy watching the many interesting pictures that emerge from the cards under your gaze.

If you look more closely and allow your imagination to roam, you will see still more pictures, all of them fascinating. Creatures are the second most commonly seen pictures in the cards. You may see cats, horses, pigs, butterflies, birds, and even mythological beasts such as dragons, phoenixes, and unicorns. At this stage, don't worry about the symbolic meaning of your visions — just enjoy the process of allowing your imagination to unfold. This, in itself, is very therapeutic.

As your thinking becomes more fluid, you may start to see all sorts of interesting landscapes and scenes. You may see castles and fantasy landscapes or industrial scenes, houses, rivers, and forests. Allow your imagination to play and see how it creates increasingly exotic environments. Gradually other pictures may emerge, such as boats, windmills, rings, towers, flowers, and so on. Everyone sees something different, and each picture says something about you. The pictures you see are symbols of your innermost thoughts and a window to your unconscious mind.

Improving Your Ability to "See"

....

SOME PEOPLE find it easy to see pictures in random shapes and can see something the moment they look at a card. For others it takes a little work, but with practice the eye tunes in to the task and the pictures soon start unfolding like a movie. Below are a few useful tips describing the many different ways that you can look at the cards. They will soon improve your ability to "see."

LOOK AT THE WHITE SPACES

As well as looking for pictures in the black ink, look at the shapes made by the white areas. A white area surrounded by black ink may easily form a negative silhouette of a picture. Also, look at the areas where white and black meet. At these contours, the outline of the black ink forms pictures. Now let your attention jump between the shapes you see in the black areas and those you can see in the white areas. The same contours can generate an array of different images.

LOOK AT THE DETAILS

The overall shape of the inkblot may create a picture such as a face or a butterfly, but it is possible to see pictures in any part of the inkblot. Try looking at smaller areas of the card for shapes and pictures. Once your imagination is activated, you will be able to see images in even the smallest details of the cards.

LOOK AT THE SUBTLE TONES

The subtle washes in the white and gray areas of the cards are one of the best areas to focus the attention.

These cloudlike areas can reveal very detailed images that you may initially have missed. Hidden in the stains are some of the most interesting images.

TURN THE CARD AROUND

Once you've had a good look at the card, try turning it upside down or on its side. You will be confronted with all sorts of new shapes, and completely different pictures will be revealed. This fresh look at the cards can stimulate new images very quickly.

LET IT HAPPEN NATURALLY

The key to seeing lots of images is to enjoy what you are doing. Try playing the inkblot game with children to see who can identify and describe the most pictures. Also, try working with other random shapes. Look at the clouds or the gnarled bark of trees for strange faces and shapes. See what pictures reveal themselves when you look at the patterns in sand, or in a pile of crumpled clothes.

Preparing to Use the Cards

....

A LITTLE PREPARATION will greatly increase your ability to use the cards and enable you to gain the full benefit. Accessing the intuition is easy if you get yourself into the right frame of mind. You need to be relaxed, yet alert. Just as the intuitive powers spontaneously manifest during sleep or meditation, so will they while you are using the cards.

STEP 1

PREPARING YOUR ENVIRONMENT

Set aside a special time to work with the cards and choose somewhere where you will not be disturbed or distracted by noise. As part of your ritual, you may want to light a candle and burn some incense to set the contemplative mood. Also, choose a comfortable chair or sit on the floor propped up by cushions. It is important to be as comfortable as possible.

STEP 2

DEEP BREATHING

This is one of the easiest ways to relax. As you take a deep breath in think to yourself: "I am …," and as you breathe out: "… relaxed." When you breathe out, allow your whole body to relax. Sink into the pleasure of being so completely at ease.

STEP 3

DEEP RELAXATION

Now imagine the feeling of relaxation

spreading through your whole body. Imagine a warm sensation in your toes and feet that spreads upward, relieving any stress. You may notice that your shoulders become relaxed, and that any pressures fall away – particularly around the eyes. Deeply relax. And feel how good it is.

STEP 4

IMAGINATIVE MEDITATION

Once you are completely relaxed, the mind slows down and becomes at ease. Let go of your worries and notice how your imagination is beginning to activate. You may see pictures and images arising in your "mind's eye." Allow the moving images to come and go. Now draw them toward you and let them become exceptionally vivid. Try not to fall asleep but remain in this state between waking and sleeping. The more you relax, the more vivid the images become. The sensation is a bit like dreaming, although you are wide awake.

STEP 5

COMING AROUND

Remain in this visionary state for as long as you wish. When you feel ready, slowly bring yourself back to normal awareness. However, allow the fluid state of awareness that you have experienced to permeate your waking consciousness. Your imagination is now active, you are more in tune with your unconscious, and your intuition is ready to work.

EXPERIMENT 1:
Tuning in to Your Intuition

....

NOW YOU are going to work with the cards in a targeted way. You will be asking the intuition for a symbol that reveals guidance about your life in general. Approach the exercise in a good frame of mind, and avoid cataclysmic questions such as "Should I leave my partner?" Once you understand what your intuition is telling you, use your discrimination to decide whether it's a sensible option.

STEP 1

SELECT A CARD

Once you have completed the preparation exercise (*see pages 58 to 59*), draw one of the cards from the pack at random. Close your eyes and relax for a few moments. Feel the breath become quiet.

STEP 2

ACTIVATE THE IMAGINATION

Hold the card in front of you, or prop it up if you prefer to sit in a

40

meditation posture. Let the imagination become active. Allow your thoughts to wander, but keep bringing them back to the card.

STEP 3

STUDY THE SHAPES

Don't try too hard. Let the mind drift and allow the pictures to form spontaneously. Look at the shapes made by the inkblot but also observe the negative shapes made by the white paper. Turn the card upside down or sideways to see what other shapes are formed. Look for images in the smallest details of the inkblot. Gaze at the page and watch what appears as your eyes go out of focus.

STEP 4

FIND THE DOMINANT SYMBOLS

After a while, one or two images are likely to seem more dominant than others. Decide which ones these are and make a note of the pictures that seem most relevant.

The images you have experienced are symbols of how you feel and what your intuition is guiding you to do. In the following pages, you will learn how to decipher these symbols using the Dictionary of Symbols in Part 3 of this book and your own skills of interpretation.

The Meaning of Symbols

IN THE experiment on the previous pages, your intuition gave you some images through the cards. These images are symbols that have arisen from the unconscious, insights directly from your intuition. They express your feelings, and your hopes and fears. By understanding the secret meaning of the symbols you can discover more about yourself, and find new ways to approach your situation.

WHAT DID YOU SEE?

Interpreting the images you see in the cards is a similar process to interpreting the symbols of a dream. Both come from your unconscious mind and give insights into the hidden aspects of your life.

You are likely to have seen a number of faces in the cards. A face is the most common image that the mind will make from a random shape. What was the face like? Was it happy, sad, fearful, or confused? Maybe it looked angry. The expression on the face may be saying something about your current state of mind or about the attitude of those around you. If you see an angry face, it may be because you are harboring hidden feelings of resentment toward someone or something. A puzzled expression might illustrate how confused you are at the moment, whereas a tranquil face can show a good attitude, the attitude you should be striving to achieve.

WHAT DOES IT MEAN?

In the same way, consider every image you see and ask yourself what it says about you. Supposing you see an anchor: an anchor stops a ship from drifting with the tide. We call people who support us "anchors." If our life feels like it is drifting, we need an anchor to hold us steady, such as a partner, a job, or a home. It's clearly a symbol of stability, although, of course, it could say that you might want to travel by sea.

Animals are also a likely image. Ask yourself what they symbolize about you. A dog, for example, may represent an actual dog, as well as the animal's qualities of friendship,

domesticity, and loyalty. A ferocious dog could symbolize your fears or uncontrolled instincts. Interpret each image as a metaphor for your life.

The Dictionary of Symbols in Part 3 lists some common images and their meanings. These are only a rough guide to symbolic meanings. It is important to interpret the images in your own way in order to understand the unique personal messages revealed to you by your intuition.

Symbols and the Mind

....

S YMBOLS ARE a universal language which teaches and preserves permanent basic truths. They are a form of shorthand for ideas and concepts. This is especially true of religious concepts, the philosophies of which have been protected from enemies by their translation into symbols. Symbols can resonate in the depths of our being and put us in touch with the fundamental human values that should govern our life.

THE LEVELS OF THE MIND

Symbols connect us with the divine part of ourselves, the part that knows all the answers to the problems we face, and can teach us the lessons that we must learn from life. Symbols can reach through all the levels of the mind, from the conscious to the unconscious.

Part 1 of this book described the fourfold hierarchy of the mind (*pages 22 to 25*): the conscious mind, the preconscious, the personal unconscious, and the collective unconscious. The first three levels were proposed by Sigmund Freud; the fourth was added by Carl Jung. I believe that a fifth level, which could be called the "transcendent unconscious," contains information received from beyond the mind by paranormal means.

LEVEL 1

THE CONSCIOUS MIND

Some of the images that you see in the inkblot are likely to have been imposed by the conscious mind. For example, you may not like a picture you see and consciously try to change it into something else. Or you may only look at the obvious shapes and ignore the more subtle images that

44

leap out when you give your imagination free rein. Consciously imposed images do not come from the intuitive mind, but they may say a great deal about you. If you find yourself trying to change an image into something more preferable, ask yourself why. What are you trying to avoid?

LEVELS 2 & 3

THE PRECONSCIOUS AND PERSONAL UNCONSCIOUS

Many of the symbols that appear on the cards represent your own personal problems, hopes, wishes, and fears. Occasionally, the pictures may remind you of past hurts, childhood worries, or repressed feelings. You may be shocked by what you see in the cards. You may see violent scenes, explicitly sexual scenes, or scenes of pain and despair. Do not be alarmed by these. Symbols often exaggerate the truth in order to bring unconscious aspects of yourself to your conscious attention. By

recognizing these unconscious forces you are taking the first steps toward solving your inner worries.

LEVELS 4 & 5

THE COLLECTIVE AND TRANSCENDENT UNCONSCIOUS

From the deepest levels of the unconscious we receive images that help us to find the means to heal ourselves and solve our problems. You may see images in the cards that show you how to correct your behavior in some way, or that offer advance warnings of emotional tensions that may soon get out of hand. On a deeper level still, the images that arise may come from the divine, transcendent part of you. These visions, captured by the cards, come from the highest source and will leave you feeling mentally and spiritually inspired. Some of the symbols may reflect the way that you are preparing yourself for clairvoyance and spiritual revelation.

Symbols and Your Experience

W E ALL ·have symbols in common – images that occur in myths, dreams, religions, and cultures all over the world. Symbols are flexible, however, and can mean different things to different people. They fit in with your unique experience. To understand what a given symbol means to you, it is important to work with the image and allow it to reveal the meaning that is personal to you.

pictures you see in the cards represent aspects of yourself.

For example, suppose you see a crying face – this may mean that you are crying inside. Perhaps you have emotional worries that are upsetting you more than you dare to admit. To discover these associations, ask yourself the following questions. Then listen to your inner voice to see what you are given in reply.

WHAT THE SYMBOL SAYS ABOUT ME

Your personal associations with the symbol are more relevant than the traditional meanings. Most of the

WHAT FEELINGS DO I ASSOCIATE WITH IT?

Notice how the symbol makes you feel. Your emotional response to it may reveal a great deal of information about your present state of mind. The symbol may highlight feelings that need to be expressed.

IS IT A PUN?

The unconscious will often use a play on words to express an idea. Suppose that you see a shape in the cards that resembles a bottle of wine. Perhaps this is a pun, warning you that you are complaining and whining too much. Jokes can be wisdom in disguise.

CAN IT TALK TO ME?

An imaginary dialogue with the symbol will help to reveal its meaning. Suppose that you see the image of a horse: close your eyes and imagine that the horse can talk. Now see yourself asking the horse for its meaning. In your imagination, let the horse tell you what it symbolizes. This fantasy technique can be used with most symbols to establish a dialogue with the image.

DOES IT REMIND ME OF SOMETHING?

Perhaps the emotions you are experiencing now remind you of emotions from the past. Your intuition is giving you a clue to your true feelings about a person you know or a situation you are in. Are the feelings happy or sad? What do they relate to? Have the courage to accept what you are being shown. You may need to make some changes in your life.

EXPERIMENT 2:
Programming Your Intuition

....

THE INTUITION is like an incredibly powerful biological computer that we have forgotten how to use. Most people panic when they have problems. Problems create more problems, and soon life is so complicated that you do not know how to deal with your difficulties. The inner computer overheats as you frantically punch the "help" button. Clearly, the intuition cannot do its job in these conditions.

HOW TO BEGIN

In order to program the intuition to answer questions, you must first disentangle yourself from your worries and calm down.

Give yourself permission to stop worrying. Let go of your emotional attachment to problems. Relax and keep it simple. Now identify one issue that is troubling you and deal with this one first.

HOW TO ASK THE QUESTION

The way you word your question is important, because your unconscious will respond accordingly. For example, you may be worried about whether you should change your job. However, in the "back of your mind" there are actually other concerns. Will a drop in wages cause money problems? Will a new job entail moving? Will you need to retrain? A direct question such as "Should I take the new job?" may not receive a clear answer. The job may be fine if

48

you don't mind moving, but it may also cause financial difficulties.

A less specific question would be better. You could ask: "What are my true feelings about changing jobs? What do I really want to do?" In this way, you are asking the intuition to help you analyze your motives. You must be sure about what you really want before you can devise practical methods to achieve the goal.

For this experiment, you are going to program the intuition to answer your question. Rather than asking for specific "yes" or "no" answers, you will encourage the intuition to generate symbols and images to help you find a solution. You are about to draw upon the incredible creative power of the unconscious.

These techniques are reminiscent of the ancient Greek oracles that used dream incubation to receive messages from the god Hypnos. Today we recognize that what the ancients called gods are in fact symbols arising from the unconscious.

STEP 1

PREPARE YOURSELF

Write down your question. Then close your eyes and relax. Relax very deeply and let go of any stress. Notice how the breath slows down and the mind becomes quieter. Feel the relaxation spread upward through your body, relieving stress. Deeply relax, more and more, and notice how good you are feeling. Let the shoulders relax, and feel the tension around the eyes falling away. Let your mind float in that wonderful state between sleeping and wakefulness. Your mind is fluid, yet you are fully alert.

STEP 2

SELECT A CARD

Still retaining your relaxed state of
awareness, open your eyes and
randomly draw a card from the pack.
Your intuition is already preparing
answers to the question you've asked.
Now look at the card and see the
pictures emerge. Remember to look
for the shapes within the white areas
as well as within the inkblot itself.
Allow yourself to enter the dream-
like state that you experienced in the
intuition experiment on pages 40–1.
Let go. Relax. Enjoy your fluid state
of awareness.

STEP 3

WATCH THE
IMAGES EMERGE

At first, don't worry about trying to
remember or interpret the symbolism
of the images. Let them emerge naturally and unimpeded. After about five
minutes, or whenever you feel ready,
make a few notes about what you
saw. You are likely to have seen

faces. Make a note of these but also
make a note of the animals, scenes,
and other pictures that you saw.
Also write down any associations
that come to mind with each picture.
Don't forget to include both the
good and bad feelings inspired
by the images.

STEP 4

INTERPRET THE SYMBOLISM

The images that you have noted
down can be interpreted in the same
way that you would interpret a
dream. They are messages from your
intuition that reveal your true feelings
– your hopes, fears, and motivations.
What do the symbols say about the
issue you've asked about? How does
this session make you feel? Are your
thoughts focused on the question
initially asked, or are you now
thinking about something else?
Perhaps you have overlooked something. Is your unconscious alerting
you to other areas of your life that
need your attention?

You may want to read The Meaning of Symbols again (*pages 42 to 45*) to help you unravel the messages, or to look at the Dictionary of Symbols. However, it is your interpretation that counts. Let your intuition guide you to the true meaning of the symbols. They are a visual manifestation of your inner voice.

STEP 5

PUT YOUR DISCOVERIES INTO PRACTICE

A grain of practice is worth a mountain of talk. Write down a sentence or an affirmation that sums up what your intuition is telling you. You may want to note down a few keywords to act as memory joggers for the days ahead. Start integrating into your life the guidance that your intuition has given you. You do not have to make sweeping changes. Little changes, applied consistently, are the most effective. Not only do the cards give you insight into you and your problems, they are also a key to your long-term spiritual growth. Use them to awaken the voice of your conscience and to connect you with the core human values that lie within you.

51

EXPERIMENT 3:
Recalling and Interpreting Dreams

O NE OF the best ways to deal with a problem is to "sleep on it." During sleep, our intuition is at work solving our problems and offering us solutions. Dreams are the intuition's way of communicating with our conscious self by using the language of symbols, metaphor, and allegory. If you can understand the meaning of your dreams, you can identify your motives, strengths, and weaknesses.

A ROUTE TO THE UNCONSCIOUS

If you work regularly with the Intuition Cards, your dreams will naturally become more vivid and alive. Making a conscious effort to discover the hidden processes that are happening within you will attune you to the unconscious part of yourself. Your dreams will extend your work with the inkblot experiments, solving your problems as you sleep.

When you look at the cards, you may be reminded of dreams you have had. Similarly, you may dream about something associated with some of the pictures you saw in the card experiments. Dreams and the cards are both doorways to the unconscious and to the wisdom that comes through the intuition. When you sit and watch images come and go in the cards you are, in effect, dreaming while wide-awake. The cards are dream mirrors. What you see in the cards is a dream unfolding and, just like a real dream, it will give you an insight into yourself. Working with the cards as well as with your dreams will help you to make the best decisions about the issues that affect your life.

DREAM SYMBOLS

Dreams can be a form of self-expression. Their symbols say a great deal about you and the way that you feel. For example, if you dream about being chased, this may be because you are running away from a problem. It may illustrate that you are refusing to face up to something about yourself or your circumstances. Similarly, if you dream of falling, this may indicate that you are anxious and feel that you have lost your sense of equilibrium in life. The dreams are saying that your situation is *like* falling or *like* running away.

In the same way, the pictures in the cards draw parallels with the way that you feel about your life. When you are given an image, compare it to some of the dreams you have had. If you regularly note down your

dreams in a dream diary, you may want to compare them with the images you have been receiving through the cards. If you notice similarities, consider why certain images recur. What do they say about you and the way you are feeling?

USING THE INTUITION CARDS

Dreams can be infuriatingly difficult to recall. Sometimes your conscious mind can only hold on to a half-remembered snippet, or you remember the dream you had just before waking but forget the dreams that you experienced during the night. Many people have great difficulty recalling any dreams, although scientists have demonstrated that everyone dreams, every night. With a little effort you can ensure that you remember your dreams every morning. The best way to remember a dream is to keep a notepad beside your bed and write your thoughts down as soon as you wake up. If you do this every morning, you will soon get into the habit of recalling your dreams. The Intuition Cards can also help you to remember your dreams.

STEP 1

PREPARE YOURSELF

Put the Intuition Cards and a notepad and pen beside your bed before you retire. Make sure that you have something to lean on and adequate light, so that it is easy to make notes as soon as you wake up. The conscious decision that you want to have a dream increases the likelihood that you will remember your dreams when you wake up. As you get ready to go to sleep, tell yourself: "Tonight I will remember all my dreams."

STEP 2

IMMEDIATE RECALL

If you wake up and remember a dream, write it down at once. First write down words you remember and things that were said in the dream,

because verbal information is the most easily forgotten. Don't worry about grammar or the order of events – just try to get as much material down on paper as you can.

STEP 3

GRADUAL RECALL

If you find that you cannot remember a dream when you wake up, lie in the same position for a while and allow yourself to drift between sleeping and wakefulness. Continue to relax, allowing your mind to "float." This will give your intuition a chance to draw a dream to your attention. Do not think about the events ahead and start planning today's "to do" list. Allow a dream to come to you.

STEP 4

USING THE CARDS FOR RECALL

If you remember nothing at all about your dream, reach for the cards. Keep your attention on the objective of remembering your dreams, and remain in a state as close to sleep as possible. Now look at the cards and allow the pictures to form. You will notice that pictures come more easily when you are in a sleepy state. Don't worry about trying to interpret any of the images you see: you are only looking for pictures to jog your memory about your dreams.

STEP 5

LETTING THE CARDS SPEAK TO YOU

As the pictures form, you will be reminded of similar pictures from your dreams. The cards will act as a sounding board, and the images revealed will be very close to those experienced in your last dream. The more you allow your imagination to work with the cards, the more of the dream you will remember.

STEP 6

DIGGING DEEPER

Even if you were fortunate enough to experience immediate recall, you may have missed many details. Look at the cards and think about your last dream. Do new pictures jump out of the page? Do they remind you of anything else from your dream? The cards will act as catalysts, prompting you to remember the dreams you had that night.

55

EXPERIMENT 4:
Overcoming Creative Blocks

....

ANYONE WHO works in a creative profession will know that there are times when the ideas just don't come. Often these blocks happen at the worst possible time, such as when there's a deadline to meet. The more pressure you're under, the harder it becomes to produce a creative solution. Fortunately, the cards can help you to get into a favorable state of mind for creative thinking.

LETTING IDEAS COME

The best ideas come to us when we least expect them to. We may wake up in the morning with a brilliant idea, or something may come to us when we are driving a car or washing the dishes. It's often when we temporarily stop worrying about a problem – when our mind is distracted by a banal task, for example – that our intuition provides us with the ideas that we've been struggling to find. Often the best solution is just that: to put the problem aside for a while and let the unconscious mind continue working in the background. Once its work is done, at the right opportunity the answer will occur to you.

UNLOCKING CREATIVITY

The cards can be used to create this opportunity. On the following pages you will use the cards as part of your creative thinking processes. By taking time out to work with them, we give ourselves a temporary respite, an emotional vacation in which we can enjoy a contemplative state of mind. It's at this time that the intuition can communicate with the conscious mind.

Half the battle in overcoming creative or intuitive blocks is to break the routine tension of your thinking. You could achieve similar results if you took a short stroll or spent more time looking at the glorious beauty of nature. However, if you work for an advertising agency, a research and development department, a newspaper, or a design house, it is unlikely that the boss would appreciate your absence. In these situations the cards can be used as a necessary distraction to get you into a more contemplative state. You will quickly be able to achieve the relaxed and fluid state of mind that is essential for creative thinking.

THE INTUITION CARDS

Using the Intuition Cards should never be a struggle. Let them become an opportunity to open the door to a more relaxed and contemplative state of mind. Look forward to using them and enjoy the results. By using the cards to inspire creative thinking, you will enjoy a fascinating experiment with the imagination. This experiment can be done at any time but is particularly useful to anyone engaged in a creative occupation. If you work on a computer and need to take regular short five-minute breaks, the cards are an excellent way to use this time.

The experiments you have tried so far have identified images in the cards, then interpreted them as symbols arising from the unconscious. This experiment is less targeted and should be used purely as a means of stimulating a creative flow of thought. In effect, it is a form of daydreaming, but with a serious purpose. Everyone has hidden creative powers, and these powers are easy to stimulate. Turn the page to begin to use your unconscious to awaken your latent powers.

STEP 1

PREPARE YOURSELF

Close your eyes and relax as you did in the other experiments. Let your mind float in that wonderful state between sleeping and wakefulness. Your mind is fluid yet you are fully alert. There is no need to set a specific

problem to be solved. The objective of this exercise is to get you into a more creative state of mind in order to perform more effectively whatever task you have set yourself – an idea for a new project, the plan for a new painting, or developing a character for a novel, for example. Once you achieve the right mental condition the ideas will come easily.

STEP 2

SELECT A CARD

Randomly choose a card from the pack, or choose one that you feel drawn to. Look into the card and see how the pictures arise. As before, look into the white areas and into the details, and remember to turn the card upside down and on its side to see whether any other pictures are formed.

Don't worry about remembering the images that occur. In this instance you are not going to interpret them.

STEP 3

ENCOURAGE FANTASY

As the images arise, let your mind make up a fantasy about what you see. Let an imaginary play unfold. For example, if you see strange faces, make up a story about the people. Why do they look the way they do? What sort of people are they and what are their hopes, fears, and ambitions?

As well as the characters, let landscapes appear. Set the characters in the landscapes; imagine the situations that unfold. At first you will need to make a deliberate effort to create stories, but once the imagination is activated, tales will unfold naturally. Many great novelists have described being able to unleash a creative stream of thought. The Intuition Cards will enable you to tap this same inner resource.

STEP 4

APPLY YOURSELF TO YOUR GIVEN TASK

Exercising the imagination in this way frees you from the restraints of conventional thinking. By the time you've finished, your head will be filled with all sorts of ideas. Now, when you apply yourself to your set project, ideas will come more naturally. The cards may have suggested some ideas already, and you are now in the right state of mind to achieve the desired creative results. You are thinking in a wholly new way. With practice, you will enter this state of mind spontaneously.

Using the Cards in Everyday Life

THE OBJECTIVE of this system is not only to use your intuition when you are working with the cards, but also to allow your intuitive powers to influence every aspect of your life. You can listen to your intuition all the time. If you can learn to trust your intuition and follow your gut feeling about a situation, you are taking the first step towards using extrasensory perception in everyday situations.

LETTERS

You've applied for a new job and you receive a handwritten envelope in reply. Close your eyes as you hold the letter and observe any pictures that appear in your head. What feelings do you receive about the sender? Are they happy? Look at the cards and see what pictures are shown to you. Psychics call this technique "psychometry," and you may find that your clairvoyant impressions prove to be correct. The cards can only give you part of the answer, but you are extending the scope of your intuitive powers.

RELATIONSHIPS

ESP works best if you like the people you're working with. And if you *love* them the powers become even more enhanced. People who are in love can finish each other's sentences and have the same thoughts. Try comparing your dreams with those of your loved one – you may be experiencing the same dreams and resolving problems together. You may also see similar images in the cards. Using the cards increases any awareness of ESP between you and those who are important to you, and can help you to trust your feelings.

HEALTH

Psychic powers can be used to heal sick or troubled people. If you see something in the cards about someone's health, send healing thoughts immediately after the session. You are already linked to that person's vibration, so it is easy to extend this and send healing light. Imagine the person well and happy, and picture your thoughts as a healing ray of light that bathes him or her, washing away problems and replacing them with powerful, living light. Wherever you send a thought of love, healing energy follows.

IMPRESSIONS

Trust your hunches. When you meet someone for the first time, notice your immediate reaction. Do you like that person? Are your hunches later proved to be accurate? Use your intuition to guess lottery numbers, the number of candies in a bag, or the name of the next person to telephone you. With regular practice your intuitive ESP will increase.

DIRECTIONS

Learn to trust your sense of direction. Put away the map and trust your intuition. You'll be surprised to discover that your intuition will take you to your destination with uncanny accuracy. At first, you'll make many mistakes, but you'll soon be able to find even the most obscure places without any knowledge of the area.

Accessing Your
Extrasensory Perception

PSYCHIC POWERS are a gift latent in everybody. In times before language, they could have been used to warn of danger, or to help with bonding or communication. Clairvoyant abilities to "remote view" distant locations may have helped to find new sources of food or water. Dowsing skills might have been inherited from these times. Precognition – the ability to see the future – would have aided survival.

DORMANT POWERS

Nature gave us psychic skills to help us to protect ourselves and evolve. We are now going to use the Intuition Cards to put us in touch with these forgotten powers.

When your imagination creates pictures in the cards, you are getting in touch with the hidden part of yourself – the unconscious mind. Here, you will gain access to the dormant psychic powers used by humankind in prehistoric times. The cards reveal your inner self, but the images are also reflections of information revealed by paranormal means.

Many of the images you see arise through clairvoyance. They provide information not just about your inner self but also about your future. Psychic techniques often work by simply demanding of the unconscious an answer, and then trusting the information given. Usually the first thought that comes to you is the right one. The skill is in sorting out which thoughts are your own and which ones come from outside of you.

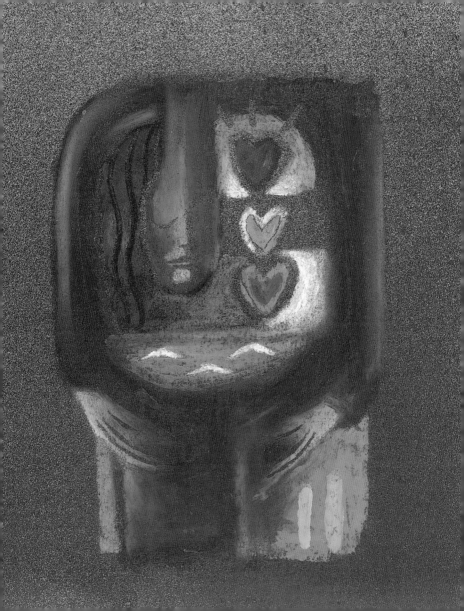

EXPERIMENT 5: Predicting the Future

FORECASTING THE future is risky. Sometimes a psychic can get it right with uncanny accuracy – at other times a psychic can make big mistakes. Often, the correct information is received, but the wrong interpretation is given. Ancient Greek stories tell how King Croesus of Lydia asked the Delphic Oracle about the impending war with Persia. He was told: "If you cross the Halys River a great nation will fall."

GETTING IT WRONG

The king went to war, crossing the river with confidence, but his army was slaughtered in battle. A great nation did fall – but it was his own!

GETTING IT RIGHT

Random oracles were once used as a means of telling the future. The pictures seen in the sacrificial fires, the entrails of animals, or the patterns in sand all revealed insights into what the fates held in store. The first shamanic priests must have relied entirely upon their own psychic intuition to determine the meaning of each individual image. Indeed, this is by far the best way to work because it directly involves the psychic powers.

However, as the oracles developed, traditional meanings were given to specific images. Many of these meanings are still used in tea-leaf reading and other traditions. Inevitably, different authors have given different interpretations of each symbol, and now many of the original meanings have been lost. Now that you have worked with the psychological meanings of images, you can begin working with their mystical meanings using the Dictionary of Symbols in Part 3. Please use these interpretations only as a guide. Your own inner hunches and gut feelings will give you the most accurate insights. Trust your intuition.

Clearly, it is important when using any divination technique to remember how easy it is to misinterpret what we "see." It is better to consider our insights as potentials and opportunities, rather than unalterable fate.

The objective of this experiment is to gain insight into your potential future. Regard the information you receive as a map that will help you avoid any pitfalls and lead you to the best possible outcome.

STEP 1

PREPARE YOURSELF

Relax and get yourself into the right frame of mind, as you have done for previous experiments. Relaxation increases the alpha waves from the brain that aid ESP.

STEP 2

ASK A QUESTION

Set yourself a target by thinking about an issue that you would like to address. Keep your question fairly open. The cards will not be able to give you "yes" and "no" answers. You are going to let them give you suggestions for future scenarios and solutions to problems. Suspend your disbelief and let reason have a holiday. What you are given from the unconscious is the stuff of genius.

STEP 3

SELECT A CARD

Choose a card at random and search it for images. Once again, remember to look at both black and white shapes as well as the small details. Allow the pictures to unfold and involve yourself in whatever fantasies come to mind. As you did with the creative experiments, let miniature dramas unfold. Are you seeing potential outcomes for the future?

STEP 4

ASK FOR ANSWERS

You may see happy or sad scenes. Remember that these are all potential events. Try to dig deeper and ask your own inner voice to guide you. What should you do to get the best result from your current circumstance? Be silent within for a few moments and answers will come to you. Your psychic intuition is trying to help you. You have only to let it come through.

STEP 5

FIND THE DOMINANT SYMBOLS

Inevitably, the cards will keep drawing certain images to your attention. Once you have decided which are the most important, you can look these up in the mystical meanings listed in the Dictionary of Symbols.

STEP 6

NOTE DOWN ANY ADVICE

When you have come to your
conclusions about what the future
potentially holds, write down a
simple message to yourself outlining
the most positive approach to take.
Carry this with you to remind you
how your intuition has advised you.

For example, angry faces in the
cards may indicate the root cause of
the next problem you will face. You
could arm yourself in this case with
an affirmation such as: "I shall
conquer anger through love." In a
similar vein, if the faces you saw
looked depressed, you could affirm:
"Happiness is my birthright."

Reading the Cards for Others

··

SOON YOU are going to learn how to use the Intuition Cards to give a reading for somebody else. However, before you do this it is important that you consider your motives and decide how you can use the cards to help people. Unfortunately, there are many fortunetellers working today who do a great deal of harm and cause much unnecessary heartache through their lack of a basic code of conduct.

68

RESPONSIBLE READING

Remember that many of the things you see will be symbols. For example, if you see macabre images, don't immediately assume that this is a prediction of a death. A genuine psychic knows that it is not possible to predict death – this is information that is denied us. Similarly, don't tell a person to go against a doctor's advice or you'll not only be in trouble with the law but may also put someone at risk.

Also, don't let your ego get in the way – the more you boast, the more your psychic skills shrink away. Be confident of course, and you can joke about how good you are, but don't take your ego too seriously.

It is also a mistake to make exaggerated claims. You are just starting to develop your skills so make certain that your sitter understands this. You can't guarantee to solve problems. Try to be as clear as possible and let it flow. When your stream of psychic impressions stops, say so, and finish the reading. It's no good just making things up to fill in time when nothing comes to you. It is better to give just a little quality clairvoyance than a great deal of nonsense.

It is also important to get the sitter into a good mood when you work. The other person's energy is as important as your own for a successful session. Instill optimism, and try to see beyond bad events to better times. Help the sitter to overcome obstacles, and stress that the sitter has the free will to influence the future. Together, you will find ways to encourage good fortune.

Strive to dig deeper with your clairvoyance. Discipline yourself never to be satisfied with what you give. If you get something correct, try adding more and being even more specific. A really good tip when you're stuck is to make your sitter laugh. Humor is indispensable to good clairvoyance. Once a person smiles or laughs, the barriers come down and the clairvoyant energy flows between you.

Receiving Thoughts

···

THE INTUITION CARDS predict the future by interpreting a random event. Carl Jung called the law that governs this process "synchronicity" and stated that "anything done at a particular moment in time has the qualities of that moment in time." His theory, in simple terms, proposed that psychological events run parallel to material ones. Hence, the powerful unconscious psyche attracts unusual coincidences.

ONE-CARD READING

The Intuition Cards are a focal point for the powerful forces of the unconscious. When you give a reading for another person, your own unconscious mind is acting as a channel. For example, you receive a telepathic thought from the person and it is expressed in one of the images that you see in the cards.

It is best to keep your sessions light, particularly when you first start using the cards. As you become more skilled you will discover that they are a powerful psychic tool. In this reading, you will use one card.

You can give a general reading, unless the sitter prefers to focus on a particular issue. If the sitter asks you to pose the cards a question, keep it simple. For example: "Tell me if my son will marry Jenny, or Sally who he left three times" would be better put as "Tell me about my son." The second question gives less away.

STEP 1

Chat with your sitter for a little while to relax him or her. If the sitter starts telling you about the nature of the problem, ask him or her not to. It's *your* job to tell *the sitter* these things.

The less you know about the person, the better. You should have no preconceptions: this isn't guesswork.

STEP 2

Ask the sitter to draw a card and hand it to you. Watch the pictures unfold just as if you were using the cards for yourself. Relax and let your mind flow. Watch for the shapes that appear in both the black and the white areas.

STEP 3

As the pictures appear, interpret them in terms of the sitter's predicament. For example, you see a house. You might say: "I feel you are thinking about a move," or possibly: "I feel you are searching for domestic security." Listen to your gut feelings. Your intuition will know what each image means.

STEP 4

The images you see reveal everything about the person's current psychological state and life situation. Further images will reveal what should and shouldn't be done about them. Your intuitive powers may also contain predictions for the potential future.

Past, Present, and Future Reading

·······································

O N THE PREVIOUS pages, you learned how to give a one-card reading. Here you will learn to use a simple spread. Using more than one card will help you to identify which images refer to the past, present, and future. This method will help you to target your psychic intuition. Once again, chat with your sitter and help the person to relax before selecting the cards for the reading.

STEP 1

When you both feel ready, ask the sitter to draw three cards from the pack. You can decide whether to let the sitter choose from face-up or face-down cards. The person can then select any cards he or she feels drawn to, or choose them at random.

STEP 2

Ask if the sitter wants a general reading or would prefer to address a specific question. Again, keep it fairly open, so that you are not unduly influenced by any suggestion in the question.

STEP 3

Lay the cards on the table in the way indicated opposite. Unlike tarot cards, it does not matter which way up the Intuition Cards are.

STEP 4

Pick up the card from the "past conditions" position and examine it. The images that come to you will relate to the past influences that created the present conditions. Your psychic intuition may also give you information about the sitter's distant past, and even his or her childhood. If so, tell your sitter about it, even if it's not relevant to the immediate issues you are dealing with. It is important to give the sitter information that he or she can qualify. If you can describe the past and present situation correctly, you are more likely to get the future right.

STEP 5

Now pick up the card from the "present conditions" position. Your sitter may be eager to know the future, but spend some time with this card so that your psychic intuition can fully involve itself in the issues that need to be addressed. Just hearing someone talk about and recognize a dilemma can be therapeutic for the sitter. Again, you will need to interpret the pictures you see as symbols of the sitter's experiences.

STEP 6

Finally, pick up the "future conditions" card. If your psychic intuition has correctly described the past and present you can feel confident that what you see for the future will also be correct. Remember, of course, that you are being given symbols, and each one needs to be interpreted. Make sure that you do this with sympathy for any suffering that your sitter has experienced, and offer kind words; you are here to help – not to frighten – the sitter.

Card 1: Past conditions
This card represents the influences that are passing away or have caused the situation.

Card 2: Present conditions
This card represents the sitter's present circumstances and the nature of the problems confronting him or her.

Card 3: Future conditions
This card refers to the potential outcome and trends. Your advice may help your sitter to avoid pitfalls and move toward good fortune.

Designing Your Own Spreads

THE INTUITION CARDS are a flexible system of oracle that can be adapted and changed according to your needs and preferences. You can devise your own ways of laying out the cards to suit you, or to answer specific questions. As long as you keep to your chosen spread, the laws of synchronicity will ensure that randomly drawn cards correspond with the conditions marked by the card positions.

A clairvoyant may use one of the Intuition Cards to give a preliminary intuitive reading to help him or her to establish a link with the client. The cards can also be useful in helping psychic intuition throw light on a tarot card that seems incongruous with the rest of the cards in a spread. The Intuition Cards are ideal for use with the Chinese oracle, the *I Ching*. The cards will give your unconscious mind a means of focusing its attention and help you to interpret, through pictures, the hidden meaning of the words of wisdom given to you by the oracle.

THE FIVE-CARD SPREAD

This spread can be used to give a more detailed view of the future.

Card 1: Past conditions

Card 2: Hidden influences with a bearing on the present

Card 3: Present conditions

Card 4: Near future

Card 5: Distant future

THE ONE-YEAR SPREAD

This spread predicts for the year ahead. Start your interpretation from the current month, and interpret card one as you did in the one-card reading on *page 71*, but without the use of prediction. The cards for the months ahead can be read one at a time, in sequence, to build up a picture of the year ahead.

Card 1:	Card 3:	Card 6:
The current	March/April	September/
situation		October
	Card 4:	
Card 2:	May/June	Card 7:
January/		November/
February	Card 5:	December
	July/August	

THE RELATIONSHIP SPREAD

In this spread, the cards represent the sitter and the sitter's current partner. Remember to advise your sitter that this is intuitive guidance, not necessarily prediction.

Card 1: The sitter – how the sitter feels about the current relationship

Card 2: The partner – how the sitter's partner feels about the sitter

Card 3: The sitter's environment – the influences surrounding the sitter

Card 4: The partner's environment – the influences surrounding the partner

Card 5: The outcome – possible solutions to resolve problems or to plan a reconciliation or parting of the ways

Developing the Inner Voice

···

THE INTUITION PACK is designed to put you in touch with your inner voice. The cards, in themselves, do nothing. You are simply using them as a way of getting in touch with the psychological and spiritual forces that we call the intuition. Since ancient times, wise people have been guided by their inner voice. Today, most people have lost touch with their inner voice and feel at the mercy of their troubles.

THE STILL, SMALL VOICE
Sometimes wisdom comes through dreams; at other times it manifests itself as the divine voice, from the angels or from God, that has inspired prophets and saints throughout the ages. Whether the inner voice that reveals this wisdom is merely the unconscious processes at work, or whether it is indeed inspired by supernatural powers, is open to debate. Certainly, it appears that the powers of extrasensory perception can unfold when you listen to the still, small voice within. For some people, the inner voice speaks with words; for others, the language from within comes in pictures or sensations.

76

Many mystical traditions, such as anthroposophy and some forms of Buddhism, believe that the inner voice is the divine "overself" communicating with us. It is the part of ourselves that has never been born and lives outside of time and space as we understand it. This overself is all-knowing, and it understands the reasons why we suffer and the purpose of our life on earth. Sometimes it interrupts our routines to give spiritual guidance. By listening to it we draw closer to our spiritual heart and further away from the base desires and pettiness of the lower self.

THE VOICES OF ANGELS

Other traditions, such as spiritualism, spiritism, and theosophy, claim that the inner voice comes from spiritual beings who live on a higher dimension of existence – spirit guides or angels. Spiritualist mediums believe that these discarnate beings can influence our thoughts and give us direct guidance about what to do in our lives. All we have to do is still the mind during meditation or quiet reflection and the spirit beings will draw close and share their wisdom with us.

The highest of all the intuitive voices is the conscience. Most of us have a sense of right and wrong, and it seems that this knowledge has not been learned from experience. It is a perennial knowledge that arises in every generation. It is the innate knowledge of what is right.

Some say that the conscience is the voice of God transcending all cultural barriers and creeds. It is the source of universal knowledge and has unlimited wisdom. Everyone possesses it. It is what Hindus call the heart. All we have to do is to be humble enough to listen to its inner prompting and we will do the right thing in every situation and grow into better people. The Intuition Cards are a way of harmonizing with this wonderful inner power.

Part 3

···

DICTIONARY OF SYMBOLS

EVERY IMAGE *that appears in the Intuition Cards means something, but the same image may mean different things to different people and at different times. It would be impossible to list all of the images you might see. The purpose of this section is to offer a selection of* possible *meanings to help you make your own judgments. It's* your *interpretation that counts.*

Interpreting the cards is not difficult. You will soon master and enjoy it. Maintain a respectful attitude toward the cards, believe they have something valuable to say, and be open and honest with yourself. In many instances, you will discover that the people, faces, places, objects, and events you see in the cards represent parts of yourself. They symbolize your feelings and fears, and aspects of your personality you have not acknowledged. The cards will teach you to be truthful with yourself. Not every image you see has a profound meaning and psychological significance. Some of the pictures reflect your everyday thoughts; others may be a repetition of the day's events.

Every entry in the Dictionary of Symbols has two sections: a psychological meaning and a mystical meaning.

The psychological meaning *tells you what the symbolism of the cards says about you and your state of mind. The images you see reflect your deepest emotional responses to your waking-life experiences. A correct interpretation of the cards' symbolism will only be possible if they are viewed in the context of your outward life. This will include your current fears, hopes, ambitions, and so on. The cards may also refer to your past and to deep-seated attitudes from childhood. They may reflect hates, prejudices, fears, guilt, and habits. By becoming aware of these qualities, you will get to know yourself better and enable your unconscious mind to cooperate with you. You will start to take control of your life and determine your own future.*

The mystical meanings *of the images are taken from traditional superstitions and interpretations found in tea-leaf reading, pyromancy, scrying, and other systems of divination. They are traditional omens and predictions for the future. Again, you must make your own interpretation of the true prophetic meaning of each symbol. Don't get too serious or literal. Have fun with these, but when it comes to true clairvoyance you will need to turn to your own inner powers of interpretation and prophecy.*

People, Faces, and Parts of the Body

EARS

Psychological meaning: Listen to what people are saying. You may be missing some very good advice.
Mystical meaning: Unexpected news.

EYES

Psychological meaning: Eyes represent your spiritual state and your perception of the world. They indicate how you see things and interpret situations.

Mystical meaning: You will overcome difficulties if you take great care in all your dealings.

FACES

Psychological meaning: Faces are one of the most likely images that you will see in the cards. Often they will appear distorted, but consider the expression. Does it say something about your state of mind? You may have feelings of repressed anger or resentment, or you may harbor hidden fears. The face may remind you of someone you know – what does this person represent about your own personality?

ANGRY FACE

You or someone around you is angry.

HAPPY FACE

Have you found happiness, or is happiness your goal?

SAD FACE

A predominance of sad faces may indicate that you are more depressed about an issue than you care to admit.

WEIRD FACE

Don't be worried by strange faces – you're not about to go mad. Faces can be made out of many shapes. Think about how the emotions expressed by the face make you feel. Your emotional response may reveal the answer to your question.

LOVER'S FACE

If the face reminds you of someone you know, then consider what bearing this person has on you.

They could represent an aspect of your own personality.

YOUR OWN FACE

If the image reminds you of yourself, you may be worried or concerned about your own self-image and how the world sees you. It can also indicate that you are able to see or understand yourself from another's point of view.

CONFUSED FACE

This may highlight your own inner confusion about what to do.

FRIGHTENING FACE

Get behind the image and find out what it is that frightens you. Perhaps you are afraid to express your true feelings, or feel insecure in some way.

TWO FACES COMMUNICATING

This may simply indicate the need to communicate your ideas to others, or your desire to express what you are feeling.

Mystical meaning: One face indicates a change, but many indicate a party. Pleasant faces foretell happiness and prosperity; unpleasant faces indicate loss. Seeing a stranger's face indicates a change of residence.

HAIR

Psychological meaning: Tangled hair can indicate a personal difficulty; straight hair indicates that you are managing to sort a problem out.

Mystical meaning: There is a whole fortunetelling system based on hair. Luxuriant, long hair denotes continued health and prosperity. Frizzy or short curly hair indicates the opposite.

HANDS

Psychological meaning: These are a symbol of dexterity and skill, and of self-expression. Depending on the gesture, they may be saying "stop," "hug me," or "goodbye," or they may be beckoning you to something new.

Mystical meaning: If the hand is outstretched, someone close to you needs help. If hands are clenched, expect a surprise.

HEADS

Psychological meaning: These may represent your behavior. A large head may represent intelligence or egotism. A square head may suggest a conformist, and a shrunken head may suggest feelings of inadequacy.

Mystical meaning: New opportunities.

JUDGE

Psychological meaning: This could represent your conscience or worries about a conflict with authority.
Mystical meaning: Setbacks and hardships.

KING

Psychological meaning: The masculine side of your nature; can also represent the intellect.
Mystical meaning: A powerful ally.

LOVERS

Psychological meaning: Lovers can have many meanings. On one level they can represent your thoughts about your personal relationships, on another the union of opposites within the psyche, such as reason and intuition. Also inner harmony.
Mystical meaning: Happiness and contentment.

POLICEMAN

Psychological meaning: Are you feeling guilty about something?

Mystical meaning: You have a secret enemy.

TEETH

Psychological meaning: According to the trance psychic Edgar Cayce, teeth and tongues are symbols for too much talking. Loose teeth may indicate careless talk, whereas crooked teeth can indicate bad language or slander. Teeth falling out can indicate hidden anxieties.
Mystical meaning: Seeing teeth or a tongue brings good luck.

QUEEN

Psychological meaning: The motherly side of your nature, or the guiding intuitive self.
Mystical meaning: A helpful friend.

VIOLENT IMAGES

Psychological meaning: You may need to express your emotions in a natural, gentle way.
Mystical meaning: Considered to be a good omen.

Creatures

....

BIRDS

Psychological meaning: A symbol of
transcendence. Consider the type
of bird that you see: a dove may
symbolize peace to come, a raven
deceit, and a peacock may warn you
to beware of pride. Birds can also
symbolize the spiritual transformation of the soul.

Mystical meaning: Troubles between
people will soon be over; unexpected
journeys. Birds with beautiful
plumage are considered a fortunate
image, bringing wealth and happy
marriages. A wounded bird foretells
troubles ahead for your children.

BUTTERFLY

Psychological meaning: Transcendence
and rebirth. This positive symbol
indicates that you are feeling inspired
and fulfilled.

Mystical meaning: You may fritter
away money in frivolous pursuits.

CAT

Psychological meaning: Normally
associated with female qualities, the

cat may symbolize the female part of yourself – your intuition, perhaps, or your psychic self. Cats are also associated with good fortune, and could indicate a good period ahead.
Mystical meaning: A false friend causes a quarrel.

CROCODILE

Psychological meaning: Hidden fears lurk below the surface of awareness.
Mystical meaning: You should beware of an enemy.

DOG

Psychological meaning: Dogs indicate devoted friendship. In myth, a dog often acts as a guide – sometimes symbolizing the wisdom of the intuition. Violent dogs may reveal your anger and a desire to express hidden resentment.
Mystical meaning: Faithfulness or envy. Seen at the top of a card, the symbol represents faithful friends; seen at the bottom, it represents extreme jealousy.

DONKEY

Psychological meaning: You may feel overworked. A donkey symbolizes gentleness; a mule indicates stubbornness.
Mystical meaning: You must be patient and optimistic.

ELEPHANT

Psychological meaning: Inner strength and wisdom; distant memories.
Mystical meaning: A symbol of lasting success and the removal of obstacles.

FISH

Psychological meaning: A universal symbol of fertility, with the promise of personal inner growth.

Superstitions say that to dream of catching a fish means that good fortune will come your way.
Mystical meaning: Successful events to do with water. Fate may call you to a distant place.

HORSE

Psychological meaning: Untamed emotions – even sexual ecstasy. Horseshoes, of course, are a well-known symbol of luck.
Mystical meaning: A galloping horse indicates good news from a lover. If you see only the head of the horse, you are likely soon to experience romance.

LION

Psychological meaning: Confidence or pride. Also a symbol of the self.
Mystical meaning: Good luck with people of high rank. Be careful of people who may be envious of your success.

MONKEY

Psychological meaning: A trickster figure. It can represent the lower mind – the bad side of yourself that sometimes gets the better of you.
Mystical meaning: Beware of a person who will flatter you.

OWL

Psychological meaning: You will gain greater wisdom.
Mystical meaning: There will be gossip, scandal, and failure.

PIG

Psychological meaning: Are you being stubborn and "pig-headed"? A symbol of selfishness and a brutish nature.

Mystical meaning: You will have material success but emotional problems.

RAT

Psychological meaning: An aspect of yourself or others that probably frightens or disgusts you. There could be problems ahead.
Mystical meaning: Treachery is afoot.

SNAKE

Psychological meaning: A sexual symbol, and a symbol of transformation or healing.
Mystical meaning: The emblem of falsehood and enmity. In some systems it can represent triumph over an enemy.

SPIDER

Psychological meaning: You may distrust others. Be careful about entering formal agreements – you may get trapped.
Mystical meaning: This indicates a determined, yet secretive person. It can also indicate money coming.

TORTOISE

Psychological meaning: This may represent your outer personality – the persona you hide behind. However, seeing a turtle indicates that an unusual incident will bring great joy.
Mystical meaning: You will be unfairly criticized.

ZOO ANIMALS

Psychological meaning: You feel caged: you may feel your life is hemmed in.
Mystical meaning: Generally, an omen that you will be freed from your difficulties. In particular, seeing a zebra indicates travel and perhaps an unsettled life.

Places and Objects

BRIDGE

Psychological meaning: A transition to new things. What do you see lying beyond? Is it a happy landscape or a foreboding one? You may have some good times ahead, or some difficult decisions to make.

Mystical meaning: An opportunity for success.

CHURCH

Psychological meaning: The sacred side of you will be of importance.

Mystical meaning: Disappointment.

DOOR

Psychological meaning: The opening to a new area of your life is indicated; there is an opportunity ahead. Is the door open or closed? This may reveal your attitude to the new opportunity.

Mystical meaning: Something strange may occur.

GARDEN

Psychological meaning: Inner peace and harmony.

Mystical meaning: You have good and consistent friends.

HAT

Psychological meaning: Your role in life. Perhaps a change of role is indicated.
Mystical meaning: A new occupation.

HOUSE

Psychological meaning: A house can represent you or your body. Its state of repair indicates your physical or psychological health.
Mystical meaning: A period of contentment and security is coming.

KEYS

Psychological meaning: A problem will be solved and you will be opening the door to opportunity.
Mystical meaning: New opportunities.

KNIFE

Psychological meaning: Someone may mean you harm, or you could have a self-destructive tendency.
Mystical meaning: Lawsuits, broken relationships, and divorce.

LADDER

Psychological meaning: Progress in spiritual or worldly status.
Mystical meaning: A happy union.

MOON

Psychological meaning: The moon has always been linked with fertility. It is associated with the tides and also with the ebb and flow of emotions, so it may suggest emotional growth. It may also predict travel overseas.
Mystical meaning: A love affair (particularly if it is a new moon).

MOUNTAINS

Psychological meaning: A quest, and obstacles to be overcome.
Mystical meaning: Obstacles or high ambitions.

PATH

Psychological meaning: The direction you are taking in life. Any other symbols you see near this image may indicate things to come. For example, if you see a face near the path it may reveal a person who will become important to you; a house may indicate a move; and a boat or a vehicle suggests a journey.

Mystical meaning: Shapes that suggest paths or roads indicate a journey.

REVOLVER

Psychological meaning: Do you feel angry about something? Perhaps it is a play on words, indicating that you will get another "shot" at an opportunity.

Mystical meaning: Trouble and quarrels lie ahead.

ROSE

Psychological meaning: Love and enlightenment. Other flowers seen in the inkblot can indicate the unfolding of something positive in your life or the development of your potential.

Mystical meaning: Ancient systems of fortunetelling say that flowers, particularly the rose, foretell great success in the arts and sciences. For couples, a rose can also indicate healthy children.

TRAIN

Psychological meaning: The direction of your life at the moment. Be careful that you don't miss an opportunity. *Mystical meaning:* It was believed that symbols of traveling indicated a change in your fortunes. It is particularly fortunate if the destination is in a straight line and toward high hills or mountains.

TREE

Psychological meaning: Does the tree bear fruit? Is it strong like the oak? Or rotten, withered, and battered? Though trees are strong, they can bend with the wind. Perhaps you should do the same when faced with adversity?

Mystical meaning: Trees can indicate changes for the better and the fulfillment of ambitions. If small inkblots or dots surround the image, you will find your success in the country.

WINDMILL

Psychological meaning: A symbol of work or of plenty. It may show how the wind of fortune drives your life.

Mystical meaning: Success comes only through hard work.

Myths and Magic

ANGEL

Psychological meaning: Your desire to become more spiritual or to rise above the commonplace. As an omen for the future it augurs well, and peace may come to you. The angel of death may be a premonition of someone dying or an indication that your attitudes must go through a death and rebirth.

Mystical meaning: A forecast of good news ahead.

DEVIL

Psychological meaning: This represents the negative side of your personality, such as feelings of envy, greed, lust, anger, hatred, and so on. It may also represent the things that you fear.

Mystical meaning: Evil influences and betrayal.

DRAGON

Psychological meaning: An evil dragon may represent your hidden fears – fears that block the way to the treasure of self-knowledge.

Mystical meaning: In Chinese oracles the dragon is a symbol of the masculine power of yang, and brings activity and creativity.

FAIRY

Psychological meaning: This represents the undiscovered side of your nature, or is perhaps a reference to your childhood. You may wish for a little magic in your life.

Mystical meaning: Most oracles consider fairies to be good omens.

GIANT

Psychological meaning: Awe-inspiring powers are dominating you or forcing you to take notice of them. Often associated with male sexuality.

Mystical meaning: A lucky omen that predicts commercial success.

PHOENIX

Psychological meaning: Rebirth. You have been through difficult times but now feel renewed hope.

Mystical meaning: A new start.

UNICORN

Psychological meaning: Power, gentility, and purity; inspiration and wonder at the marvels of the inner world.

Mystical meaning: You will have some official correspondence.

WITCH

Psychological meaning: The shadow side of yourself, symbolizing everything you have pushed out of your thoughts – the negative feelings that you refuse to recognize.

Mystical meaning: Witches are an ill-omen and indicate problems ahead.

WIZARD

Psychological meaning: A good wizard represents the higher self within you, the innate knowledge that expresses itself through your intuition.

Mystical meaning: You will experience many changes.

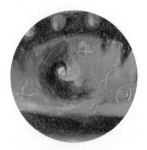

Suggested Reading

Exner, J.E. *The Rorschach Systems*, NEW YORK: GRUNE & STRATTON, 1969

Exner, J. E. *The Rorschach: A comprehensive system*, Vol. 1: Basic foundations (3rd ed.), NEW YORK: JOHN WILEY & SONS, 1993

Rorschach, H. *Psychodiagnostics*, SEATTLE: HOGREFE & HUBER, 1998

Jung, C. *The Archetypes and the Collective Unconscious*, LONDON: ROUTLEDGE & KEGAN PAUL, 1959

Hamilton-Parker, C. *The Psychic Workbook*, LONDON: VERMILION (RANDOM HOUSE), 1995

Jung, C. *Synchronicity: An acausal connecting principle*, LONDON: ROUTLEDGE & KEGAN PAUL, 1955

Index

....

angels *77, 92*

animals, symbolism of *84–7*

archetypes *23*

atomic physics *10–11*

Bleuler, E. *20*

body parts, symbolism of *80–3*

Bohm, E. *21*

Bohr, N. *10–11*

breathing *38, 48*

candles *38*

Cayce, E. *83*

clairvoyance *9, 12–13, 34*
   ESP *24–5, 74*
   inner voice *79*
   oracles *30, 33*
   symbols *45, 62, 69*

collective unconsciousness *23, 44, 45*

creative blocks *56–9*

crystals *24–5, 28*

Da Vinci, L. *22*

Dee, J. *26–7*

dialogue *47*

dictionary *41, 43, 51, 65, 66, 78–93*

directions *61*

dowsing *12, 62*

dreams *8–9, 10, 15, 19*
   meaning *42, 60*
   recalling *52–5*

environment *38*

Exner, J.E. *21*

extrasensory perception *12–13, 60–2, 65, 76*

faces *42, 46, 67, 80–3*

fantasy *59*

feelings *46–7, 50, 60*

forecasting *64–7*

Freud, S. *22–3*

geomancy *32–3*

Graves, R. *16*

guidance *9, 51, 77*

gut feelings *9, 18, 60, 65, 71*

health *61*

Howe, E. *10*

hypnotic trance *7*

I Ching *30, 74*

impressions *61*

incense *38*

inkblots *20–1, 34–5, 36–7, 41, 44, 50, 52*

inner voice *8, 19, 66, 76–7*

interpretation *41, 50–1, 64–5, 71, 73, 78–9*

Jung, C.G. *23, 44, 70*

Kant, I. *17*

Kelly, E. *27*

Kerner, J. *22*

letters *60*

95

magic *92–3*

meditation *39*

Mitchell, E.D. *12*

myths *92–3*

Nostradamus *26–7*

objects *88–91*

oracles *30–3, 49, 64, 74*

people *80–3*

places *88–91*

precognition *9, 13*

preparation exercises
38–9, 40, 48, 54, 58, 65

Presley, E. *15*

programming *48–51*

psychoanalysis *22*

psychokinesis *13*

psychometry *60*

puns *47*

pyromancy *30, 79*

questions *48–9, 65*

readings *68–73*

reason *16–17, 65*

recalling dreams *54–5*

relationships *60, 75*

relaxation *38–9, 48, 50, 54*

Rhine, J.B. *12*

Rorschach, H. *20–1, 22*

scrying *25, 26–7, 28, 79*

sewing machine *10*

Shakespeare, W. *29*

spreads *72–5*

symbols *15, 22, 23, 31*

  dominant *41, 66*

  dreams *53*

  experience *46–7*

  meaning *33, 40, 42–3,
  50–1, 73, 78–9, 93*

  mind *44–5*

  programming *49*

synchronicity *70, 74*

tasseography *32*

telepathy *12*

transcendent unconscious
44, 45

visual projection *15, 24,
28–9, 30–1*